CIVICS

Laws

By Cassie M. Lawton

Cavendish Square

New York

Published in 2021 by Cavendish Square Publishing, LLC
243 5th Avenue, Suite 136, New York, NY 10016

Website: cavendishsq.com

This publication represents the opinions and views of the author based on his or her personal experience, knowledge, and research. The information in this book serves as a general guide only. The author and publisher have used their best efforts in preparing this book and disclaim liability rising directly or indirectly from the use and application of this book.

All websites were available and accurate when this book was sent to press.

Portions of this work were originally authored by Leslie Harper and published as *How Do Laws Get Passed? (Civics Q&A)*. All new material this edition authored by Cassie M. Lawton.

Library of Congress Cataloging-in-Publication Data

Names: Lawton, Cassie M., author.
Title: Laws / Cassie M. Lawton.
Description: First edition. | New York : Cavendish Square Publishing, 2021. | Series: The inside guide: civics | Includes index.
Identifiers: LCCN 2019059400 (print) | LCCN 2019059401 (ebook) | ISBN 9781502657077 (library binding) | ISBN 9781502657053 (paperback) | ISBN 9781502657060 (set) | ISBN 9781502657084 (ebook)
Subjects: LCSH: Legislation–United States–Juvenile literature.
Classification: LCC KF4945 .L39 2021 (print) | LCC KF4945 (ebook) | DDC 349.73–dc23
LC record available at https://lccn.loc.gov/2019059400
LC ebook record available at https://lccn.loc.gov/2019059401

Editor: Kristen Susienka
Copy Editor: Nathan Heidelberger
Designer: Tanya Dellaccio

The photographs in this book are used by permission and through the courtesy of: Cover everything possible/Shutterstock.com; p. 4 Culture Club/Getty Images; p. 6 (top) Fuse/Corbis/Getty Images; p. 7 (top) Dünzl/ullstein bild via Getty Images; pp. 6–7 (bottom) De Agostini/Getty Images; p. 8 Syda Productions/Shutterstock.com; p. 9 https://upload.wikimedia.org/wikipedia/commons/6/6c/Constitution_of_the_United_States%2C_page_1.jpg; p. 10 fotog/Getty Images; p. 12 (top) Tony Savino/Shutterstock.com; pp. 12–13 (bottom) Rick Scibelli/Getty Images; pp. 13, 16 Chip Somodevilla/Getty Images; p. 14 SAUL LOEB/AFP via Getty Images; p. 15 Leonard Ortiz/MediaNews Group/Orange County Register via Getty Images; p. 18 Victor J. Blue/Bloomberg via Getty Images; p. 19 Michael Runkel/Getty Images; p. 20 (top) David Santiago/Miami Herald/Tribune News Service via Getty Images; p. 20 (bottom) mark reinstein/Shutterstock.com; p. 21 Michael Brochstein/SOPA Images/LightRocket via Getty Images; p. 22 Toshi Sasaki/Photodisc/Getty Images; p. 24 Andrey_Popov/Shutterstock.com; p. 26 PhotoQuest/Getty Images; p. 27 The Asahi Shimbun via Getty Images; p. 29 (top left) antoniodiaz/Shutterstock.com; p. 29 (top right) Richard Hutchings/Corbis Documentary/Getty Images Plus/Getty Images; p. 29 (bottom left) DON EMMERT/AFP via Getty Images; p. 29 (bottom right) Hill Street Studios/DigitalVision/Getty Images.

Some of the images in this book illustrate individuals who are models. The depictions do not imply actual situations or events.

CPSIA compliance information: Batch #CS20CSQ: For further information contact Cavendish Square Publishing LLC, New York, New York, at 1-877-980-4450.

Printed in the United States of America

Find us on

CONTENTS

Ancient societies, like the Romans, had different laws for their people to follow.

LAWS: WHAT ARE THEY?

Chapter One

Every country has different laws that the people who live and visit there must follow. Laws are official rules passed by a group of people, such as a government. They're an important part of countries and governments around the world. They tell people what things are acceptable to do and what things aren't acceptable to do. If people follow the laws, they're often seen as being good citizens. However, if people don't follow the laws, they can end up in trouble.

A Long History

For as long as people have lived together, there have been laws. Most laws are created to keep people safe. The earliest written laws that we know of are over 3,700 years old! Some of the oldest civilizations to have laws were the ancient Babylonians, Egyptians, Greeks, and Romans. Some civilizations had laws made by a king or queen. Others had laws made by groups of important people, mostly men. These groups of men were called councils or senates.

One US law states that people must tell the truth in a courtroom if they take an oath, or promise, to do so.

In the United States today, there are many laws. There are laws that say how old you must be before you can vote or drive a car. Laws tell us how fast we can drive on a road. Laws also tell us that we can't hurt others or steal. When people obey laws, it makes it easier for everyone in a community to get along!

Laws Everywhere

If you think about it, there are laws about nearly every part of life. There are laws about signs that must be posted in restaurants, such as signs reminding employees to wash their hands. There are laws for how houses and other buildings are built. The laws might explain what types of **electrical outlets** are needed, where they should be located, and how far apart they should be in a room. There are also laws to help make buildings more accessible, or easy to enter and move around in, for people who need to use a wheelchair. Other laws help keep the people who build homes and other buildings safe while they're working.

Employees Must Wash Hands Before Returning To Work

Laws play a part in our everyday lives—from how fast people can drive their cars to what signs we see in the bathroom!

Fast Fact

One of the oldest lists of laws is the Code of Hammurabi. Hammurabi was a king in ancient Babylon, over 3,700 years ago. His code described 282 laws for his people.

School Laws

Laws also play a part in the things that happen at schools. For example, a law might say you can't have a weapon in school. Another one might say you have to go to school until you're at least 16 years old.

The US and state governments create many laws for many different parts of life. It's important to follow laws to be a good, active citizen.

Fast Fact

Laws passed by the US government are called federal laws. Examples include laws that control immigration, or the entry of people into the country.

Laws for schools protect students and teachers.

THE US CONSTITUTION

The most important set of laws in many countries is called a constitution. A constitution is a group of laws for the whole country. The US Constitution was created in 1787 during a meeting of representatives that's now known as the Constitutional Convention. Today, it's a model for many constitutions around the world. The US Constitution outlines the different parts of the US government and what they can and can't do. It also includes other laws, called amendments, that have been added to the Constitution since it was created. The first 10 amendments, called the Bill of Rights, were added in 1791. They talk about a citizen's main rights. Some later amendments have helped people who didn't have all their rights in 1791. For example, women couldn't vote in the country until 1920, when the 19th Amendment was passed.

Fast Fact

There have been 27 amendments to the US Constitution as of 2020.

The Constitution is the United States' main set of laws.

Lawmakers in the US government meet in the Capitol Building in Washington, DC.

WHO MAKES THE LAWS?

Chapter Two

All laws are made by people. These people often are part of an official group. The group will talk about the law when it's just an idea, and then they vote on whether or not to pass the law and make it official. Everyone in the group has a different opinion and a different **role**. They work together to make sure a law is right.

Local and State Laws

Some laws apply only to a small area, such as a city or a county. Local governments, such as a city council, make these laws. Local laws usually concern matters such as where you can park a car or how late at night you can make loud noises. They might also say when public parks in your community can be open or closed.

State laws apply to an entire state. The group that makes these laws is called the state legislature. Members of the legislature listen to the people of their state, then pass laws based on what those people want. That's why something may be legal in one state but illegal, or against the law, in another state. For example, some kinds of gambling are legal in some states but not in others.

Fast Fact
Congress is the name of the legislature of the US federal government.

In the winter, local laws say which side of the street cars can park on. That helps snow plows make one side of the street clean so cars can later park on it.

Federal Laws

In the United States, the federal government is divided into three branches: executive, judicial, and legislative. The executive branch carries out laws. The judicial branch interprets laws through the courts. The legislative branch, or US Congress, makes the laws.

Congress is made up of the Senate and the House of Representatives. These two sections are called houses. Each house has a certain number of members. In the Senate, members are called senators. There are two senators from each US state. Members of the House of Representatives are called representatives. Each state has a different number of representatives according to its population. States with higher populations have more representatives.

Congress passes many laws every year. These federal laws apply to everyone in the United States.

Fast Fact

Some laws, such as speed limits, differ from state to state. Texas has some of the highest speed limits in the United States.

Shown here is a meeting of representatives.

Leaders of the Legislature

The House and Senate have different leaders who help make laws. The leader of the House of Representatives is the Speaker of the House. The leader of the Senate is the US vice president, who is also part of the executive branch. If a vote in the Senate is tied, the vice president will cast the final vote to break the tie. Both the vice president and Speaker of the House are important parts of the legislative, or lawmaking, process.

In 2020, Senators Chuck Schumer (*left*) and Mitch McConnell (*right*) were the Senate minority leader and the Senate majority leader, respectively.

Fast Fact

When **initiatives** make it onto a ballot for people to vote on, many states call them propositions. Each proposition is given a number. If enough people vote for a proposition, it becomes a law. Other states have different names for initiatives. For example, they may be called proposals, questions, or issues.

In addition to the Speaker of the House and the vice president, there are several other people who have leadership roles in Congress. Two examples are the Senate majority leader and the Senate minority leader. These roles are divided according to the political party in Congress that's in power. For example, if a majority of senators are from the Republican Party, the Senate is being led by the Republican Party. Therefore, the Senate majority leader is a Republican. The minority leader comes from the party with fewer members in the Senate. The majority leader and minority leader must work together to bring issues concerning both parties to the Senate and to move bills—written suggestions for laws—forward.

INITIATIVES AND REFERENDUMS

In some states, laws can be voted on directly by the people. When a person or group wants a new law to be passed, they can ask people who agree with them to sign a **petition**. If enough people sign it, an initiative can be put on the ballot—a form used for voting—on Election Day. This asks voters if the initiative should become a law. The people of the state vote on it. If enough people approve it, it becomes a law.

If someone doesn't like a law passed by the state legislature, they can also try to get enough people to sign a petition against it. A **referendum** on the ballot asks people if they would like to keep, change, or throw out a law that already exists. Both initiatives and referendums are important parts of the lawmaking process.

Petitions help change laws or create new ones in communities.

President Barack Obama is shown here signing a bill.

HOW ARE LAWS MADE?

*I*n order for something to become an official law in a country or state, it must go through a special process. This process takes an idea and turns it into a law. Understanding this process is an important part of understanding how the government works.

Making a Law

Laws begin as bills. They can be basic plans for ideas, like free education or cleaner air and water. Bills can be for a particular country or state. Different groups of people write the bills, depending on which audience they're for. Members of the federal legislature write federal bills, which deal with the United States as a whole. State bills are written by state legislatures.

The main person who writes or introduces a bill is called the bill's sponsor. At the federal level, this is either a senator or a representative in Congress. Other members of the legislature who agree with the bill can also be listed as secondary sponsors, or cosponsors. Federal bills may be written in either the House of Representatives or the Senate. Most state legislatures also have two houses, often called the state assembly and state senate. No matter where it starts, a bill will go through many of the same steps. First, it will be given a number and read to the entire house. Then, it will be sent to a committee to be read and studied.

States have assemblies that help make state laws.

The Committee Meets

A committee is a smaller group of members of the legislature. Each committee focuses on a different subject. There are different committees for bills that deal with money, education, the **environment**, and many other things. Committees often call upon experts for help. The experts have studied key subjects that might be included in a bill. They're good people to consult about changes that should be made to the bill.

When a bill goes to a committee, the members of that committee read it carefully. Sometimes, a bill may have many different parts and be hundreds of pages long! The committee will research the reasons why the bill should or shouldn't become a law. They can also make changes to the bill. When they're ready, the members of the committee vote on whether or not the bill should move forward.

Fast Fact

A bill can be reviewed, or read, several times before it's ready to be **debated** and voted on.

The Whole House

If the members of the committee agree with a bill, they'll send it back to the whole house of the legislature for a vote. Each bill needs a certain number of votes in order for it to pass.

However, before a vote is taken, lawmakers debate the bill. More changes can also be made to the bill after it's been debated. Then, it's time for the vote. If the majority of the members vote that the bill should be a law, the bill has passed in that house. A bill passed in one house is then sent to the other house of the legislature, where it goes through the same process all over again.

This building is the Nebraska State Capitol, where the state's senators meet.

Fast Fact

Nebraska's state legislature only has one house. This is called a unicameral legislature. All members are called senators. This is the only US state to have such a government.

A governor signs a bill to make it a state law.

The Executive Branch

If a bill passes both houses of the legislature, it's then sent to the executive branch for final approval. The executive branch is a separate part of the government responsible for carrying out the laws that the legislature has created. At the federal level, the head of the executive branch is the president. At the state level, the executive branch is led by a governor.

When a bill is sent to the president or governor, they read it. If they agree, they sign it, and the bill becomes a law. If they don't agree, they can veto it, meaning they refuse to sign it. In this case, the bill doesn't become a law at that moment. Both houses can try to override the veto, however, and make it a law without approval from the executive branch.

Members of Congress debate a bill in order to decide if it should become a law.

EXECUTIVE ORDERS

In the United States, presidents can create and sign their own laws without going through the lawmaking process. This type of law is called an executive order. Executive orders have been delivered during wartime, during times of unrest in the country, and to protect or help groups of people or the environment. All executive orders are numbered, written, and signed. Their first publication usually appears in the federal government's daily journal, the *Federal Register*. Members of the public can see them there and learn about them. Congress doesn't approve executive orders, and it can't overrule them. However, the US Supreme Court can declare them unconstitutional, which means they go against the Constitution. There have been over 13,000 executive orders written by US presidents.

President Donald Trump is shown here signing an executive order.

Fast Fact

When a bill comes to the president, they have 10 days to decide what to do. If the president hasn't signed the bill or vetoed it after 10 days, it becomes a law if Congress is still meeting. If Congress has finished meeting for the year, the bill will "die," or not become a law. If the president vetoes a bill, Congress can decide to take another vote. If two-thirds of both houses vote for the bill, it becomes a law.

Laws keep people safe in their communities.

WHY LAWS MATTER

Laws are some of the most important parts of our society. The way they're created is important too. By having debates and taking votes, we keep the process as fair as possible. New laws can be created, and old laws can be changed or thrown out. As people's ideas and beliefs change over time, laws can change with them.

However, some laws stay the same across time. This happens when a law still makes sense in modern society. If the law ever becomes outdated, it can be **modified**, or a new law can be passed to replace it.

Fast Fact

If someone breaks the law, there are consequences, such as paying a fine. A fine is a certain amount of money paid for breaking a law. Another example of a consequence is going to jail.

Changing the Law

Whenever someone doesn't like a law, they can take action to change it. They can speak out against the law. They can challenge the law in the US court system. They can even take the fight to the Supreme Court, the highest court in the United States, for a final decision. If the Supreme Court decides that a law is unfair, the law goes away.

An example of this happened in the 1950s, when not all people were treated equally under the law in America. Many African Americans living in the South were forced to live separately from whites. They ate at different restaurants, drank at different water fountains, and even had to sit in different places on city buses. This separation was called segregation. Schools were also segregated.

The best way you can help laws change is through exercising your right to vote when you're older.

VOTE HERE

Many people didn't like segregation. Schools for African American children weren't as good as schools for white children. People worked hard for change. They brought a case called *Brown v. Board of Education of Topeka* to the Supreme Court. It argued that all children, no matter what they looked like, should be allowed to go to school together. In the end, the Supreme Court agreed. They announced their decision in 1954. Segregation in schools would no longer be allowed.

Other steps people can take to state their unhappiness about a law or issue include protesting or marching. During a protest, people gather in large groups and talk about the issue. Sometimes, they hold signs that show their opinion. One example of protesting happened in 2019 when students around the world, including in US cities, held **strikes** to demand their governments take action to fight **climate change**. If enough people show their displeasure and join together, change can happen.

What Can You Do?

Learning about laws and how they're made is an important part of being a citizen. That way, when you're able to vote for lawmakers, you can make informed decisions. The more you learn, the greater impact you can have when the time comes. A great way to learn about laws and lawmaking is to read! There are many books and articles that talk about politics and civics. There are also classes in school that you can take to learn more.

Protests like this one helped change the law and make segregation illegal in the United States.

With a parent or guardian's permission, you can also visit official government websites and lawmakers' social media pages. You can ask important questions to your members of Congress or local government officials.

One of the most powerful tools you'll have to shape how laws are made is your vote. Even though you can't vote now, you'll be able to in the future. In the meantime, you can go with a parent or guardian to see how voting is done. You can learn all you can about issues happening in your community or government and help adults who vote make good decisions. When you're older, you'll be able to vote for the people you want to make the laws. It's important to get involved now to make good choices in the future.

Fast Fact

As of 2020, only three US presidents have ever been impeached: Andrew Johnson, Bill Clinton, and Donald Trump. However, no president has ever been removed from office.

IMPEACHMENT

While presidents have the power to make executive orders, they must follow laws too. If they don't follow them, they can get in trouble. A process called impeachment happens if a president is thought to have broken a law or done something harmful to the country while in office. Members of the House of Representatives first bring an **offense** forward. If the House members vote in favor of charging the president, the president is said to have been impeached. Next, the Senate holds a trial to decide whether or not to remove the president from office. At the end of the trial, the senators vote. If two-thirds of them agree, the president is removed from office and the vice president takes over as president. Impeachment doesn't just happen to presidents, however. It can happen to federal judges too. State governments also have their own impeachment processes.

Speaker of the House Nancy Pelosi (*seated*) signs the impeachment charges against President Donald Trump in January 2020 before sending them to the Senate for a trial.

FUNNY LAWS IN THE UNITED STATES

Even though laws are important, there are some state laws that have been around for centuries that are silly! Here are a few examples:

Georgia

You can't eat fried chicken with a knife and fork.

Colorado

You can't roll boulders on public property.

Arkansas

You can't honk a car horn at a sandwich shop after 9 p.m.

Kansas

You can't screech car tires.

Idaho

You can't throw snowballs to destroy property.

Louisiana

You can't steal a person's crawfish.

Pennsylvania

You can't catch fish with your mouth.

THINK ABOUT IT!

1. Why is it important to have laws? What are some laws your community has?

2. What are some consequences of not following the law?

3. Who are some of the leaders of Congress? Why are they important?

4. How can you learn more about the legislative branch of government? How can you help voters make good decisions?

GLOSSARY

climate change: The process by which weather patterns change due to rising global temperatures caused by human activity.

debate: To discuss an issue between groups of people with differing viewpoints.

electrical outlet: A place to plug in appliances or other devices that require electricity to work.

environment: The natural world around us.

initiative: A proposed law to be voted on by the people or passed to the legislature for a vote.

modify: To change.

offense: A wrongdoing.

petition: A formal way to ask for something to be done.

referendum: The practice of submitting a question to the public on a proposed change or addition to legislative policy to have the public vote on it.

role: A part or job.

strike: A refusal to participate in something, such as school, to protest an issue.

Books

Atkinson, Sean, et al., eds. *The Politics Book: Big Ideas Explained Simply*. New York, NY: DK Publishing, 2018.

Barcella, Laura. *Know Your Rights!: A Modern Kid's Guide to the American Constitution*. New York, NY: Sterling Children's Books, 2018.

How Does the US Government Work? Newark, DE: Speedy Publishing, 2017.

Websites

Branches of the US Government
www.usa.gov/branches-of-government
This website gives information about the different branches forming the US government.

How a Bill Becomes a Law
kids-clerk.house.gov/grade-school/lesson.html?intID=17
This website goes through the different steps of a bill becoming a law.

What Is the Legislative Branch of the US Government?
www.youtube.com/watch?v=hltv8-nzcUc
This video explains what the legislative branch is, how it started, and how it works today.

INDEX